MW01006518

Forever Grateful To You:

Made in the USA
Monee, IL
06 April 2022

94225600R00066